# ETERNAL

## Tan-Ku

### Sequences & Sets

by
Mariko Kitakubo
Deborah P Kolodji

Eternal
Tan-Ku Sequences and Sets

Copyright © 2025 by Mariko Kitakubo and the Estate of Deborah P Kolodji

ISBN 978-1-7377113-7-7

Library of Congress Control Number: 2025930175

Cover image by Mariko Kitakubo

Shabda Press
Duarte, California
www.shabdapress.com

*Dedicated to my dearest soulmate Debbie*

# Contents

# Eternal Bond

*Elle est retrouvée.*
*Quoi? - L'Éternité.*
*C'est la mer allée*
*Avec le soleil.*

Excerpt from Arthur Rimbaud's poem "Eternity."

My soulmate and writing partner Deborah P Kolodji, known around the world as an excellent haiku poet, crossed the bridge to the other world on July 21, 2024, after a long battle with cancer.

I have not yet been able to recover from the deep sadness of losing my dear friend, with whom I have worked for so long as a duo—each of us the other's poetic muse.

As I have carried on our shared ambition to publish a second Tan-Ku collection *ETERNAL*, I realized that I was being protected by an amazing feeling. I felt that she was still by my side, comforting me and gently guiding me through this journey, just as she had when she was alive.

The title *ETERNAL* was born from the desire to express such eternal bonds, eternal memories, and love. Although I felt powerless, I was able to publish this collection of our work thanks to the encouragement of so many people, and above all, the support of Deborah's spirit, who is always by my side.

I would like to express my sincere gratitude to both Tanka Society of America President Michael Dylan Welch and The British Haiku Society President Iliyana Stoyanova for their wonderful blurbs.

I am thankful for the support of Debbie's family and the Southern California haiku and tanka community in which she was a beloved leader. Special thanks to Kath Abella Wilson and Sean Kolodji for their contributions bringing this beautiful book to a finish.

I would like to also thank and acknowledge Tuệ Mỹ Chúc of Shabda Press for believing in our work and publishing both of our books of tan-ku. Her support brought this book *Eternal* to fruition.

Mariko Kitakubo

## ■ On This Collection

Each tan-ku contained in this volume includes haiku and tanka verses. All haiku verses were written by Deborah P Kolodji, an American haiku master. All tanka verses were written by Mariko Kitakubo, a Japanese tanka poet.

The italics refer only to the second voice in the poem, not particularly to either one of the authors. Some of the tan-ku in *ETERNAL* start with a tanka by Mariko Kitakubo while others start with a haiku by Deborah P Kolodji. We like the look of italics for the second voice in each poem.

## ■ About Tan-Ku

Tan-ku is a new genre of poetry developed by Deborah P Kolodji, an English-language haiku poet based in the United States, and Mariko Kitakubo, a Tokyo-based tanka poet. The poetry form emerged out of their seventeen-year friendship with tan-ku poems written collaboratively online and via text messages for approximately four years prior to Kolodji's passing.

In a tan-ku poem, tanka and haiku (or haiku and, then, tanka) are woven together, alternately. Tan-ku sequences are composed of four or more verses of tanka and haiku (two or more of each type of poem in alternation), and tan-ku sets are comprised of two verses—one of each form. Tan-ku sequences and tan-ku sets are completed with a title.

Tan-ku is not written by one author, but is a combination of haiku and tanka written by two authors who have a profound connection to each other.

The first collection of tan-ku *DISTANCE* was published by Shabda Press in April 2023, consisting of work composed by Deborah P Kolodji and Mariko Kitakubo as early as 2020. The second volume of tan-ku *ETERNAL* was published by Shabda Press in 2025.

To continue to promote their poetry form, Mariko Kitakubo founded the Tan-Ku Association and began publication of *Kizuna*, the Tan-Ku Association Online Magazine. For more information, please visit the Tan-Ku Association official page or Mariko Kitakubo's website.

https://www.en.kitakubo.com/index.php/category/tan-ku_association
https://www.en.kitakubo.com

## 永遠の絆

*Elle est retrouvée.*
*Quoi? - L'Éternité.*
*C'est la mer allée*
*Avec le soleil.*

アルチュール・ランボーの詩「永遠」より抜粋


私のソウルメイト、英文俳句の世界で優れた作家として知られた Deborah P Kolodji 氏が、2024 年 7 月 21 日、癌との長い闘いの末に天に召されました。

常に二人三脚で作品を詠んできた片割れを喪い、深い悲しみから未だ立ち直ることは出来ません。
　しかしその志を継ぎ、私達二人の第二 Tan-Ku 集 ETERNAL を編むことに時を費やすうち、私は不思議な感覚に護られていることに気付きました。それは、彼女が生きていた時と全く変わらず私の傍らにいて、私を慰め優しく窘めてくれているという実感でした。タイトルの ETERNAL は、そうした永遠の絆、永遠の記憶、愛を表したい気持ちから生まれました。
　多くの英語圏の歌人、俳人の方々のお励ましと Deborah の魂に支えられ、この度出版にこぎつける事が出来ました。

素晴らしい推薦文をお書き下さいました Tanka Society of America の President Michael Dylan Welch 氏、そして The British Haiku Society の President、Iliyana Stoyanova 氏に、深く御礼を申し上げます。

出版に際しご尽力くださいました出版社 ShabdaPress 社の Tuệ Mỹ Chúc 氏にも心より感謝致します。
どうもありがとうございました。

北久保まりこ

＊ここに収められた全ての俳句は　英文の俳人、俳句マスターDeborah により書かれたもの。全ての短歌は私、日本の歌人　北久保まりこによるものです。
イタリック体は詩の 2 番目の作のみを指し、特に私たちのどちらかを指しているわけではありません。私たちの Tan-Ku の中には短歌で始まるものもあれば、俳句で始まるものもあります。各詩の 2 番目の作をイタリック体にすることで、皆様がより鑑賞しやすくお感じになれば幸いです。

■Tan-Ku について

アメリカ在住の優れた俳人で、十七年来の親友でもあるデボラ・P・コロジ氏と私が共同で創りあげた詩の新しいジャンルです。

短歌と俳句（または俳句と短歌）が交互に編まれた詩を Tan-Ku と呼び、「Tan-Ku 連作」は短歌と俳句を二作品以上、「Tan-Ku セット」は短歌と俳句を一作品ずつ組み合わせたものです。
Tan-Ku 連作と Tan-Ku セットは、それぞれタイトルを伴った形で完結します。

Tan-Ku は一人の作家が書くものではなく、互いに心の通った繋がりのある二人の作家が書いた俳句と短歌を合わせた作品です。
更に詳しい情報をご希望の場合は、"Tan-Ku Association"公式ページ、又は北久保まりこのウエブサイトへお立ち寄り下さいませ。
https://bit.ly/3ZW7JTE
https://www.en.kitakubo.com

2020 年の作品をまとめた第一 Tan-Ku 集、「DISTANCE」は 2023 年 4 月に刊行されました。
第二 Tan-Ku 集「ETERNAL」は 2025 年、シャブダ・プレスより刊行されました。

# *Evolution*

# Prehistory

what did he
stammer
that night
super blue moon
over the Balkans

*summer evening*
*the clarity*
*of my hearing aid*

sometimes
better not to know
everything...
the lilies of the field
the birds of the air

*butterflies flitter*
*flower to flower*
*dreams*

the lost
continent,
Greater Adria
transparent wings
of giant dragonflies

*plucking petals*
*from a daisy*
*my own evolution*

# Water Opal

shimmering stone
the ring no longer
on my finger

*cool comfort*
*on my bare feet…*
*searching for*
*the songs of an ocean,*
*water opal dune on Mars*

# Signs

gray drizzle
all my ghosts
come back to haunt me

*a snow white*
*bud opens*
*on a chilly but*
*pure morning…*
*sacred sign*

*Loss*

# Loss

there is
no border
between
this world and the other
eternal prayer

*his face so peaceful*
        *somewhere*
*cherry petals fall*

# What's Left Unsaid

incense smoke
his soul
hangs around
to express thanks
and goodbye…

*images of him*
*as I read the prayer card*
*whispers*

# Shinobu*

偲*

coming back
from the mourning
house—
silent shine
of a bereaved mug

*first cup of coffee*
*he used to put cream*
*in his*

Shinobu*, 偲*
means "remember the deceased" in Japanese.

# Still

the end
of the bridge
hidden
in overgrown weeds...
foggy hope

*footsteps stilled*
*on the wooden planks*
*a great blue heron*

# Mares Tails

once again
Grandma
mishears
a merry-go-round
without riders

*paint fleck*
*in a wooden horse's eye*
*loneliness*

# On the Edge of my Mind

appearing in
the parallel world
on the lake
shining ripples
stop whispering

*gentle waters*
*and yet...the wildness*
*of spring blooms*

# After He Left Us

aftertaste
of childhood
pale pink
cotton candy
on Father's Day

*cloudy sky*
*the helium balloon string*
*slips from my hand*

# Through the Torii Gate

light through trees
a swallowtail follows me
on the garden path

*waking up*
*without anxiety*
*this morning,*
*parents are smiling*
*in my dreams*

# Reaching Out

rainy week
emails for a loved one
returned
the sky so near...
where are you?

*stars hidden*
*by city lights...*
*and yet, crickets*

a few words
come down...
pure
pianissimo sounds
from a pale cloud

*ripples spreading*
*one stone skips*
*across the water*

# Remnants

streaks of sadness
across the sky
Perseids

*they were born*
*on the typhoon night–*
*picking up*
*the chipped fragment*
*of the purple crystal*

*Quetzal, a Miracle Code*

# Unmentioned Casualties

a baby moose
eats marsh grasses
invisible hope...
contaminated
Polesie**

*submarine sonar*
*700 dead dolphins*
*in the Black Sea*

Polesie** is a historical place name in northern Ukraine.

# Scarred

echoes…
birds who used to perch here
long gone

*one writhed*
*weeping willow*
*survives*
*the scorching light*
*Hiroshima*

# Release

rose scent
fills up the patio
we talk of war

*let's shut*
*and lock the door*
*against strife*
*release caged birds...*
*endless skies*

before dawn...
squawks of a hundred
wild parrots

*wind from*
*a colorful*
*homeland*
*forest nostalgia*
*Costa Rica*

new songs
I find a green feather
on the sidewalk

*quetzal*
*a miracle code*
*to survive—*
*longing for*
*a peaceful future*

# Floating Away

champagne
glass toast…
sleepless
and dreamless
tank fishes

*Brahms concerto*
*Interlude*
*bubble bath*

# Spring Rain

sweet rain
on my flower bed
I welcome home
its early spring
scent

*green buds*
*the rebirth*
*of a garden*

sakura shoots
covered with
March snow
will a painless future
be possible?

*parasites*
*the loss of an orchard*
*crop*

how many
years ago
the bloody soil
around my roots
pain recalls pain

*strife planted*
*I yearn to be rain-drenched*
*with healing*

# Sundial

this sunset
is only for today
step by step
I'll be able to
start a new life

*ocean swallowing*
*the remaining light*
*moonrise*

*Oyster World*

# Far Away Flag

long
long lines
of zodiac
me? only a tiny light
longing for the fixed star

*flags of welcome*
*and yet...*
*this wait*

# Cape May

without talk
just smiles for each other
two beach chairs
at sunset
we need nothing

*lull tide*
*two gulls skim*
*the horizon*

under
the cloud-shaped
angel,
standing on the dune
I believe in miracles

*the music of the sea*
*calms my weary spirit*
*footprints in the sand*

what
am I searching for...
following
the tracks
seabirds leave

*land's end*
*our eyes on the lighthouse*
*against the clouds*

# Pilot's Special

I can't finish
the big breakfast,
Annia's Cafe...
the tiny airport,
unforgettable sky

*sparrows scurry*
*under the tables*
*a plane's lift off*

# Flight to Tokyo

small plane overhead
your photo texted
from the check-in counter

*sitting*
*at a cozy sofa*
*still I'm*
*a California lady*
*international airport*

gulls in the sky
flying to the sea
your plane still here

*how many*
*doors and sunsets*
*will we have*
*in our days?*
*hard but beautiful lives*

boarding pass
that last step
before leaving

*star*
*born from tears*
*under*
*the bougainvillea...*
*next flight plan*

# Oyster World

air and water
separate us
without walls
glittering quietly
the magical distance

*Aladdin's carpet...*
*a startled sea gull*
*passes by*

# Passengers

changing
trains to return
home...
long railway
through grasslands

*midnight silence*
*the sound of a far off*
*air whistle*

I can't remember
the name of the bridge...
still playing
hide and seek
with mom's ghost

*bare hills*
*my mother's stories*
*about the troop train*

the door
opens and closes
so many faces...
departure bell
for my life, again

*cabernet sauvignon*
*I sit in the dining car*
*alone*

# Updraft

little by little
getting in nomad mode
again...
deep autumn color
for my nails

*plane tickets*
*to a distant place*
*migrating geese*

*Result*

# Hospital Dawn

wretched rain
my IV fluid can't
catch up

*rays of light*
*shine through*
*the clouds*
*soundless moment*
*of prayers*

# Out of Clouds

a dark cloud
gathers in my heart
why?
spring melancholy
on a fine day

*colorful blossoms*
*a bee more interested*
*in my plate of food*

# Silent Circle

chaos...
souls of previous
cherry petals
in the dark silent
solar eclipse

*seasons of life*
*I stare at the bright ring*
*of totality*

# Golden Poppies

abandoned
at the end
of the world
you are forgotten
sunshine seeds

*lashes flutter*
*as I dream*
*golden poppies*

quiet
colors of dawn
on the packet
the disabled artist
opens my eyes

*morning light*
*I reach for a pair*
*of gardening gloves*

my rebirth
in the early summer
breeze…
invisible tiny lives
in a soft lump of soil

*planted*
*in the rich earth*
*I long for your blooms*

# Spring Arrives

listening
in the middle of
a colorful storm
we dance and sing
together

*the clouds lift*
*a hundred thousand poppies*
*in bloom*

# Result

twilight state
in the O.R.
liver biopsy

*whose eyes*
*catch my cancer...*
*a pure beam*
*comes through*
*the crystal ball*

*Papyrus Boat*

# Spirit

fuzzy border
between me and the stars
African gods
appear in the air
above the baobab tree

*dancing grassland*
*his skinny arms over*
*the barrel of water*

# Kaval Notes

a young
Egyptian princess
wakes up
in the dune
with a newborn fossil

*a basket floats*
*down the Nile*
*sacred ibis*

# High Risk Delivery

hidden
behind the ripples,
history
is repeated...
papyrus boat

*hemorrhage*
*a baby survives*
*in the floodplain*

# Downpour

the door
opens just a crack
which couple
will be chosen
for the ark on the hill

*first raindrops*
*before the deluge*
*distant thunder*

# Columbia River

a raindrop
touches the river
and goes on
as the stream…
reincarnation

*mouth at the ocean*
*the salmon run*
*upstream*

*Fireworks*

# Wind Change

lonely summer
a Covid test
between us

*isolation*
*strengthens*
*our bonds*
*moonlight*
*of solstice*

no ocean to cross
a mockingbird's flight
of separation

*shine*
*of transparency*
*jellyfish*
*a crayfish rests*
*on the driftwood*

floating
in our bubbles
currents of life

*when did I*
*start to paddle*
*searching*
*my childhood*
*dreams*

# Fireworks

longing
is always lonely sky...
under
the jacaranda
fireworks finale

*far away and yet...*
*the meteor shower*
*lights up the sky*

# Tanabata

palm leaf sounds...
turquoise manicure
in midsummer
resting on the shore
bringing us closer

*your thumb as you hang*
*the tanzaku*
*our matching wishes*

# Bougainvillea

summer breeze
the daily test after
exposure

*wearing*
*pink bougainvillea*
*in my hair—*
*the negative result*
*makes me positive*

# The Heat Wave

hiding
in the bamboo shade
with a gecko
heat wave escape—
distant thunder

*pool noodles*
*we float together*
*in the coolness*

# Farmers Market

cool under
the golden wonder tree
guava juice

*hard times*
*are forgotten*
*in the shade*
*the passionate taste*
*of clock-grass*

*Leaving the Womb*

# The Change of Seasons

autumn dunes
when will I see you
again

*wind ripples*
*will reach you—*
*desert roses*
*dyed by*
*the setting sun*

# Wish List

September showers
the rainbow between
you and me

*my cat*
*misses you too*
*raising a glass*
*of sparkling wine*
*to the future*

the sun peeks
above clouds in the East
another day alone

*changing*
*the hanging scroll*
*for autumn*
*my dreams fill out*
*a billowing sail*

pea-green boat
the moon also
dancing

*a stain*
*of blueberry brandy…*
*wish list*
*in my twentieth year*
*as a wandering poet*

# Gliding

release
from gravity
back
to my previous life
diamond dust

*clear sky*
*that October day*
*outstretched wings*

## Across the Sea

feeling
the sea breeze...
I am hiding
in your shadow
on the California beach

*my face towards you*
*the tide comes in*
*goes out*

# Zoom

waiting
for you to join...
the rainy season
is always long
in my life

*slow sunset*
*a snail leaves a silver trail*
*across the leaf*

# Hubris

through
the distorted
glass
he smiles to me
from the white limousine

*blue green shimmers*
*a peacock struts*
*his stuff*

# New Parasol

dreaming...
have lunch
together
on my terrace
before roses

*sip of tea*
*I close my eyes*
*and you're here*

through
my new parasol
sunshine
pours down
on days gone by

*soft wind song*
*a hummingbird*
*drinks nectar*

sometimes
sweet and sour...
your favorite
blueberry jam
like our lives

*flowers bloom*
*in memory*
*our mothers*

# Leaving the Womb

in previous…
are you real
twin sister?
mystery mist
around the earth

*an ocean between*
*their pregnancies*
*our mothers in heaven*

# The Wait

high tide
makes me
defenseless…
ancient blue of
the Pacific Ocean

*your ship shrinking*
*into the horizon*
*I wait ashore*

# Color Wheel

who named
the color salmon pink
salmon
don't care
just go up the river

*Pike's Market*
*fishmongers*
*throwing fish*

*Visitors*

# Found

first day of winter
the street too empty
of my lost little dog

*under*
*the twilight sky*
*he catches me*
*his calm snore*
*in my arms*

# Winter Meditation

snowflake
on a weathered face
lotus position

*between*
*sky and world*
*a 700 year*
*archaic smile...*
*Kamakura*

# A Midnight Clear

listening
with half of my mind
Christmas carols...
I sit in front of
an empty chair

*distant stars*
*thinking of the broken bell*
*that never rings*

puppy
in the winter sky
the Procyon
on your heart
isn't it painful?

*keepsake ornament*
*my mother's spaniel*
*misses her too*

barking
on the gentle hill
the shepherds
still search for
a better future

*the night wind*
*sings with joy*
*newborn baby*

# Visitors

starless night
guest list for Christmas
shrinking

*sadness*
*brings fortune*
*to my front door…*
*red or white wine?*
*unexpected reunion*

# Clarity

the dream
scares me,
the star
too shiny sky high
in the winter night

*curtains closed*
*I shut my eyes*
*and see it still*

# Wonderland

snowy sun
through treetops
with snow flowers
the winter god must be
tall with his long hair

*white powdered branches*
*in a row of pine*
*sleeping mountain*

# Messenger

morning
is shining through
the clouds
white tips of wings
Saint Gabriel

*pounding horse hooves*
*when my mother delivered*
*the mail*

# 'Tis the Season

Christmas
twinkling stars
separated
like us
are we the Canis Major?

*dark night*
*the Bethlehem star*
*of friendship*

the sunrise
was 2000 years ago
will the sunset
come soon?
our mythology

*delivery package*
*to another country*
*reindeer sleigh*

following
the tiny footprints
on the snow
fairies call me
from the aurora forest

*snow angels*
*the harmony of carolers*
*resounding*

# Advent

waiting for
a box of rose wine
with the buds...
silent green of
Christmas roses

*snow tears*
*the year she had*
*no gift*

# Far North

distant sleigh bells
sinking into a dreamland
Christmas

*St. Nicholas*
*left the reins*
*in the air*
*salmon pink*
*aurora*

# Resolutions

New Year's Day
the snowdrift
still unmelted

*stirring*
*a tequila sunrise*
*with an icicle...*
*the end of 2023*
*a new beginning*

*First Sunny Day*

# A Higher Sky

more than
thirty years…
a thorny road
brings me here,
endless future

*the water shoot*
*grows taller*
*fresh rose buds*

is there
an air pocket?
swinging
high up in the sky
free flight

*starling murmuration*
*the playground*
*empty now*

a vortex
revolves around
Polaris...
sleeping cat
on top of the slide

*backyard sprinkler*
*grandchildren jump*
*over the jets*

# The Darkened Day

crying
in his small universe
the solar eclipse
won't be eternal
hand in hand

*view limited*
*through solar lenses*
*halo of totality*

# The Rain Inside

holding
his knees and weeping
Sundays
in childhood are
raining, always

*a peek of sunshine*
*the umbrella of*
*a grandmother's hug*

# In the Garden

dragonflies circling
those things we avoid
discussing

*gaze…*
*the angry red*
*through*
*their wings*
*Japanese bridge*

# Airborne

they have
their own skies
seed helicopters
under the maple tree
hammock dream

*lazy summer day*
*the drone of a small plane*
*taking off*

# First Sunny Day

under
the green canopy
of the elm tree,
time stops for a while
your welcoming smile

*discarded chrysalis*
*my disquietude*
*flies away*

# Colorado Boulevard

strangers
smile at each other
from different parts
of the Earth
2023 Rose Parade

*drum beats*
*I wave at the band*
*from Japan*

# February

morning sunshine
the snow where
you are

*invisible now*
*but I'm sure*
*sakura's*
*flowering power*
*will surround us*

# Writing a Book

pruning the rose bush
a manuscript
takes shape

*confused*
*together*
*waiting for*
*the sparkle of*
*Shunrai\*\*\**

daffodil stalks
begin to emerge
the clarity of rain

*looks like*
*a tiny purple orchid,*
*lady rosemary…*
*our dream*
*forever young*

planting a garden
arranging the bushes
by height

*birds, bees*
*a monsoon…*
*seeds*
*fly far away*
*to another continent*

Shunrai\*\*\* means Spring thunder

*for my Dearest soul twin sister, Debbie,*

*Tanka Sequence*

by
Mariko Kitakubo

...That night, 2024.7.21.
*Upon receiving the sad news...*

from the other side
of the cosmic noise
what?
I faded out,
repeating No.....

not knowing
if it's true or not
I float
in the air,
floating for a few days

what is time?
the coldness
of rocks
left behind
by rapids

still
searching for Debbie
I get lost
in the festival alley
for a while

longing
is always
lonely sky
remnants of fireworks
...darkness

*...Three weeks later...*

feeling
you so close
without
time zone or distance
buck moon night

we smile
each other
somewhere...
our footprints
on Cape May beach

freedom
from everything that
separated us...
let's write a poem
on this theme

sharing emotions
connected us always,
that reminds me
I am connected
to the universe with you

my thoughts
never stop—
are you making
this happen?
so that I don't cry

the pale colors
of the flowers
decorated
in our photos
would you like it?

why aren't you
sleeping yet?
you chide me, so
let's continue our chat
in a dream (it's 4:45am)

a wish
on the meteor shower
night…
always be with me
your soul

while
my heart is still
my heart,
while I am still me,
let me offer this prayer

why does
everyone think
you're not here?
you're here
with me now

before
I knew it,
your hand
is supporting me
as before

the boundary
between life and death
is invisible
holding hands and looking
at the beautiful horizon

# Publication Credits

Across the Sea, *Mariposa*, May 2023

Cape May, *Under the Basho*, 9 Aug. 2024

Far North, *Scarlet Dragonfly Journal*, Dec. 2023

Fireworks, *Colorado Boulvard.net*, 24 Jul. 2024

Golden Poppies, *Under the Basho*, 9 Aug. 2024

Hubris, *Rattle* 83, Mar. 2024

Loss, *#FemkuMag* 36.Sep. 2024

On the Edge of my Mind, *#FemkuMag* 36.Sep. 2024

Passengers, *Under the Basho*, 9 Aug. 2024

Prehistory, *Under the Basho*, 9 Aug. 2024

Scarred, *Environmental Impacts of War*, 2024

Shinobu, *#FemkuMag* 36.Sep. 2024

Still, *#FemkuMag* 36.Sept. 2024

Sundial, *Shot Glass Journal*, Feb. 2023

Tanabata, *Colorado Boulvard.net*, 24 Jul. 2024

The Wait, *Shot Glass Journal*, Feb. 2024

Through the Torii Gate, *Mariposa*, Dec. 2023

www.ingramcontent.com/pod-product-compliance
Lightning Source LLC
Chambersburg PA
CBHW020210090426
42734CB00008B/1002